THE STRANGE CASE OF
DONALD TRUMP

Other Works by Sandy Krolick

Вероника: Сибирская Сказка (Novel)
Veronika: The Siberian's Tale (Novel)
The Recovery of Ecstasy: Notebooks from Siberia
Apocalypse of Barbarians: Inquisitions on Empire
Conversations On A Country Path
Gandhi in the Postmodern Age
Recollective Resolve
Ethical Decision-making Styles
Культурныи критицизм
Myth, Mystery and Magic: Religion in Ancient Egypt
Russian Soul and Collapse of the West
Shambhala (Novel)
Misha (Novel)
On Being and Being Good
Q: Interpreting QAnon
A New Heaven and a New Earth
Philosophic Play
Babel Unhinged
The Siberian Shaman and Western Myth
Notebooks: Philosophical Memoirs
Expelled From The Garden
Agnosis and Parousia

THE STRANGE CASE OF DONALD TRUMP

SANDY KROLICK, PH.D.

ISLANDS PRESS
NEW YORK : ALTAI KRAI : FLORIDA

ISBN: 978-1-7350698-3-8

Cover art courtesy of:
Yuri Ivanov
Altai Krai, Russia

Around the hero everything turns into a tragedy... Friedrich Nietzsche

Trump as Mythic Hero

The fantastical images of Donald Trump that have been systematically emerging from the ranks of the Religious Right and splashed across the Internet are as frightening as they are sacrilegious. And his followers — those calling themselves the true MAGA believers — are somewhat pathetic pantomimes of the mythic hero they have magically conjured up out of whole cloth. The roots of such mythologizing may be found to lie squarely within the apocalyptic imagery and tradition of Christian faith, specifically within the *Gospel of John* as well as the *Book of Revelation*. The vital force behind this belief in Trump's mythic-heroic stature seems to rest squarely on a presumption of the coming of the Eschaton and the hoped-for reality of salvation for his true believers. In this respect Mr. Trump is viewed by his faithful like a divinely anointed Savior…

> *seen among many in the MAGA base as a flawed actor that the Christian God is using to divine ends in American politics.* (*Rolling Stone Magazine*, Tim Dickinson, July 15, 2024)

While a legion of Christian Nationalists and Evangelicals, acting much like a modern-day cargo cult, anxiously await the world-transforming eschatological event of destruction and redemption, we must step back to reflect upon the depth of the political and spiritual challenges it poses for us today. The specific orientation of these cult-like movements appears poised to eclipse the very fabric of democratic rule in the obdurate hope of bearing witness to the unfolding of their imagined sacred history, the dawning of a 'new heaven and a new earth' ruled over by their divinely sanctioned figure, a world not unlike those images from *The Revelation To Saint John*.

> *Then I saw a new heaven and a new earth; for the first heaven and the first earth had passed away; and the sea was no more. And I saw the holy city, the new Jerusalem, coming down out of heaven from God, prepared as a bride adorned for her husband. (21: 1-2)*

Now, this New Testament passage becomes the principal source of our greatest fear and overriding concern — the potential for violent political upheaval grounded in some disaffected mythic-religious zeal for the end of the world. On the other hand, for those skewed and skewered faithful, it appears that the disgraced former President now represents the incarnation of those believers' very salvific hopes. As one columnist characterized the situation earlier this year:

> *Trump's record aside, there is a more disturbing phenomenon going on among conservative Evangelicals: a Christian nationalist movement in which Trump can only be described as an irreplaceable figure whose political success is crucial to God's plan for redeeming a sinful world.* (Ed Kilgore, 'Do Evangelicals Think Trump Is Jesus?' *Intelligencer,* May 8, 2023.)

References to the former President's apparent status and his divinely sanctioned mission are now strewn across diverse press releases, articles, internet chatrooms, and even on the evening news. Just browse a sampling of the words supporting the former President. Earlier last year, around Easter week, a brief post on the blog *Gab* obliquely referencing Trump's trial reads as follows: "*Seems there was someone else who was tortured and crucified this week.*" Meanwhile, a briefer post on *Telegram* in the same timeframe was yet even more apocalyptic: "*Good vs Evil. Biblical Times. Divine Timing.*" In short, Donald Trump has attained mythological status among a not insignificant portion of the Christian faithful. Even Ben Carson, a retired neurosurgeon and Trump's former HUD Secretary, recently suggested that the assassination attempt on his former boss was just the latest in a series of divine trials.

> *They tried to bankrupt him. They tried to slander him. They tried to imprison him. Now they have tried to kill him, but if God is protecting him, they will never succeed.*" (*Rolling Stone Mag.*, Tim Dickinson, July 15, 2024)

The delusional thinking inspired by the likes of a wanna-be dictator seems as implacable as it is impenetrable. And the preachers are no less fanatical regarding such heretical ideation. As one author notes, after the assassination attempt . . .

> *Republican-leaning preachers had no problem finding the topic of their sermons; they all knew that it was 'the hand of God' that had saved Trump from death and expatiated on that miraculous intervention—boldly mixing religion with politics — and even discerning and interpreting God's motives for his intercession.* ("God is a Republican and Trump's 'Miraculous Salvation' Proves It..." *La Voce di New York*, July 15, 2024, Grace Russo Bullaro)

And while his most deluded acolytes were seen with bandaged right ears during the Republican Convention recently, imitating their own savior's mythic journey and his messianic suffering after the assassination attempt, not a few Republican allies in Congress quickly followed suit by registering their own biblically-based support. The testimonials included one from Speaker Mike Johnson: "GOD protected Trump yesterday." And there were others from Representatives Carlos Antonio Gimenez (Trump survived by "the grace of God"), Cory Mills ("divine intervention" and God's "protective hand" were there), and finally Maria Elvira Salazar whose illustration on **X** showed an angel intervening on Trump's behalf. The thorough mythologizing of this deeply disturbed and unlikely hero just keeps growing! So let's explore this idea of the former President's mythological status.

Myth-making stems from some of the earliest stirrings of human creativity, including those sacrosanct stories found in both the Old and New Testaments. Throughout prehistory and history, myths have served more or less to ground societies by anchoring individuals to their community as well as to their surrounding environs. But given their existential bearing, myths may also be interpreted as relevant to a broad array of current social or historical events — bestowing a unique status upon otherwise mundane states of affairs. And just as we may demythologize a primal narration to disclose its existential meaning, so too can historical personages or events become mythologized, bestowing upon them a special sacred status or legitimacy by means of the mythic narration itself.

In other words, we should understand that there seems to be a mythologically-charged anticipation of the return of their would-be savior, Trump, motivating Evangelicals along with their volatile brethren — the Christian Nationalist foot soldiers. And, it is precisely such faith that continues to drive a sharp wedge into the body politic of American society. This explains the odd case of Mr. Trump and his loyal following — turning the most ordinary of historical figures into a mythic hero for an inordinate plurality of Americans. And they see in the apocalyptic vision of Saint John's Revelation that which is determinative for America today (*John*, 18:4-5;7)

> *Then I heard another voice from heaven saying, Come out of her [Babylon/America], my people, so that you do not take part in her sins, and so that you do not share in her plagues: for her sins are heaped high as heaven, and God has remembered her iniquities. . . As she glorified herself and lived luxuriously, so give her a like measure of torment and grief.*

Such mythic imagination has a near limitless capacity to overwhelm present reality and create a life-world of its very own making. The subject of myth or the myth-maker may also be taken over by the persona of the mythic hero himself, living this mythical life to its bitter end. Mr. Trump and his entourage are consumed by the mythic reality that has been established. And they will now do whatever it takes to live out these mythological images, including rounding up nonbelievers, deporting naysayers, or killing infidels. Donald Trump himself has been consumed by his own mythological imagination. Because he was just a shallow, already empty shell of a person to begin with, he was able to put on this new mythological cloak, and not just play the part but become a mythic hero, now untethered and unconstrained by any convention or historical reality.

As a myth-maker, candidate Trump is the prime mover of this story, enabling his loyal followers to partake in that special status accorded to a pristine time of the origins — '*in illo tempore, ab origine*' — anchoring the present moment within a meaning-filled and foundational framework already foretold in their Holy Book.

But when the mythological imagination spills over into everyday reality triggering current events, the results can be deadly and/ or catastrophic. Recall the insurrectionists storming our Capitol following the last election cycle or, as was pointed out above, that lone gunman's attempt on the former President's life. Myth has the capacity to inform current reality in ways that, while impactful, frequently go unnoticed and, more often than not, unheeded. Emerging from the unconscious within a largely fabulous and deeply symbolic framework, myth has a visceral impact on its believers with real life effects on their current perception of reality.

Letter To The Trump Faithful

Well, the courtroom drama has all but ended, and the man with the bright orange mane has been convicted by a jury of his peers. All that remains in the administration of justice is sentencing of the felon which is slowly but surely approaching. Consequently the man with the bright orange mane has gotten his panties in a royal bunch, and he is now on a full-throated revenge tour. It seems that not a day goes by without hearing the word 'retribution' escape the former president's lips, or seeing it strewn among his various public posts, as well as those of his adoring acolytes.

His principal concern, if reelected, is neither with governing the country nor guiding our Republic forward. Rather he is consumed only with exacting revenge on his accusers and inflicting retribution on his perceived enemies. These are his goals in the current election cycle; no one should be fooled into believing otherwise!

Of course, even as Trump hawks his new digital trading cards or — perhaps more importantly — his recently minted *God Bless The USA Bible* for sixty dollars a pop, our convicted felon has never himself cracked open any part of that sacred Holy Book. I guarantee you — not even once! So he would not at all be familiar with the words found in *Deuteronomy* 32:35. Likewise, we can be certain he has no inkling that this divine command is reiterated in Paul's *Letter to the Romans* (12:19) where the apostle quotes the identical Old Testament scripture: "Vengeance is mine, I will repay, says the Lord."

Here the Apostle Paul clearly commands the faithful not to avenge themselves, not to be overcome by evil, but rather to overcome evil with good. Of course this assumes there was some evil perpetrated by the jury's verdict which is clearly not the case. But more to the point, we read in *Leviticus* (19:18)

> *You shall not take vengeance or bear a grudge against any of your people, but you shall love your neighbor as yourself…*

Yet those same unwashed masses of Christian faithful, stepping in line with the Trump playbook, continue to believe and assert that he is a new incarnation of their salvific hero, and that he has the right to exact retribution for his prosecutions — while ignoring the historical Jesus' direct call for forgiveness and for the faithful to love thy enemy or turn the other cheek. The calamity baked into such demagoguery would be laughable if it were not so dangerous, fraught as it is with the prospect of deadly political violence (recall the J6 prelude) and the potential for dismemberment or destruction of the union. Not since the Civil War has America been this close to prospective chaos and likely catastrophe.

Those blind followers of convicted felon Trump — not a few of them likening the situation to Jesus' trial before Pontius Pilate — seek to unravel the very threads of our democracy in order to install their once and future king now as dictator. After all, any number of Trump loyalists have roundly asserted that his court appearance came during Christianity's most sacred time, Holy Week, when the faithful commemorate their Lord's crucifixion and resurrection. As one believer posted on the far-right microblog *Gab,* "Seems there was someone else who was tortured and crucified this week." Comparisons of Trump and Christ now run rampant among the MAGA faithful, many firmly believing that he is a martyr, following the lead of one congresswoman who directly linked Trump's prosecution to the persecution of Jesus.

Yet the convict continues his abuses undeterred by either law, shame, or civility. He even admitted — yelling to his supporters in Nevada recently — "I don't care about you. I just want your vote. I don't care." The man could not have been any clearer; he cares not for the people — just their votes. And this is all aimed at saving himself from more trials and potential prison sentences while persecuting and and vowing to prosecute his enemies. He is moving us ever closer to a dictatorship run solely on vengeance and retribution. Those who are with him will be saved (perhaps with a few exceptions), while those who are against him will be cast out into the darkness.

How can such a dark figure like felonious Trump be revered as champion of Christian values, and held up by the most diehard of the faithful, when he has such a sordid history of sexual abuse, financial crimes, and other assorted legal and business misdeeds. I imagine it is just one of those divine mysteries! But never forget this: convicted felon Trump does not care about you! He just wants your vote… and your money!

Trump's War On America

As if we have not yet heard enough whining from this man called Trump! With or without the State and Federal indictments, there is always more for him to bitch about. But the indictments have raised a far more dangerous specter. It's not simply a matter of his off-handed ejaculations before a microphone; nor is it just an issue of his corny simple-mindedness or his downright ignorance. In fact, there are some who feel that his machinations and off-the-wall comments are diligently pre-planned and flawlessly executed events, in short, that there is a strategy to his apparent madness. And perhaps those holding that view are correct. But, I just could not see any reason behind his displays of vanity and puffery, until I finally realized that such proclamations of his were intended for a very specific audience.

Certainly, the issue of his grand ego rises to the surface first and foremost, with Trump believing that his needs alone should demand appeasement. He will not entertain the thought that other persons are real actors as well, with needs of their own. There is a rigid irrationality to this monomaniacal view he holds of himself. Perhaps we can understand this posturing more fully by recalling what the Roman Emperor Caligula expressed in his own personal motto: "Let them hate me, so long as they fear me!" Or, perhaps we should just repeat the words of Trump's own messianic message: "I am the only one that can save this nation." And he utters these words as he calls for his faithful to be there for 'the final battle'. Again, we are faced with the apocalyptic visions and the threat of Armageddon as disclosed in Saint John's *Revelation*, Chapters 20 and 21.

Of course, while Trump still tries to raise the specter of an autocracy bearing down upon us from the political Left, we clearly see that it is a dictatorship from the Right that he presents without shame or denial. And his non-stop name calling — 'Crooked Joe Biden,' 'Deranged Jack Smith,' 'Lying, Crazy Kamala' — is a strong indication not only of the demonization of his rivals, but an alarmist detachment from reality. One Trump defender, posting in *The Donald*, an online forum that helped promote the January 6th insurrection, asks: "Why are we talking about anything but dragging the political elite out of their homes and setting them on fire?" This is the psychopathy with which we must now deal directly and without inhibition. There is no more brushing this stuff under the rug.

Trump's sickness is like a phoenix that has died only to rise again; and, as before, now it has taken hold of a not insignificant portion of the extremists on the political Right. We must be and remain vigilant! Do not turn a blind eye to the messianic madness that is fueling the apocalyptic vision of his supporters, including some very warped Christian evangelicals. When they call for the Eschaton, or the End Time, as they are doing, we need to be wary and to be prepared. Remember, he has called this . . . The Final Battle!

www.ingramcontent.com/pod-product-compliance
Lightning Source LLC
Chambersburg PA
CBHW071940020426
42331CB00010B/2956